The Magic of
Talk

with

Ben Franklin

A Journey of Self-Improvement and Discovery

Rich Davis, Ph.D.

MerryMount Publications

The Magic of Talk with Ben Franklin

Copyright © 1994 by Rich Davis

All Rights Reserved. Printed in the United States of America.

Permission to reproduce or transmit in any form or by any means, electronic or mechanical, including photocopying and recording, or by an information storage and retrieval system, must be obtained by writing to:

> MerryMount Publications
> Post Office Box 6428
> Asheville, NC 28816

Library of Congress Catalog Number
93-091764

International Standard Book Number
0-9639122-9-1

Rich Davis is available for training and speaking presentations. This book is offered at a special rate when ordered in bulk quantities. Write MerryMount Publications or call (704) 251-2628.

To my friends in Blue Ridge Toastmasters
Club #8215

"A true Friend is the best Possession"
–Ben Franklin

Acknowledgements

Thanks to the following people for providing help, encouragement or support with this project: My wife Ginger, Lona Rosenfeld, John Erwin, Betty Davis, Roberta Greenspan, Wilma Hamlin, Joe Cerminaro, Sharon Bares, Carl Granados, Carl Nyberg, Deborah Compton, Stacy Keith, Cindy Conner, Andrew Craig, and the hundreds of smiling faces in the audience that have given Ben and Rich a warm sense of appreciation.

Contents

Foreword   7
Introduction   9
1   The Miracle of Madeira   11
2   The Magic of Talk Pyramid   17
3   Self-Communication   21
4   One-to-One Talk:
    Making People Talk   25
5   One-to-One Talk:
    Improving Your Talk   29

6	Talking in Groups	33
7	Talking Before Groups	37
8	The Five-Week Plan	41
9	Walk in Beauty	55
10	Make Them Glad They Talked With You	67
11	Improving Your Talk	81
12	The Magic of Mixing	97
13	Magical Public Speaking	111
14	Thoughts on Self-Talk	121
15	In Conclusion: Rich	131
16	In Conclusion: Ben	135

Foreword

It is with great pleasure that I have contributed to this unique project. I realize that as an authority I am slightly out of date, which is why I solicited the help of Dr. Davis in bringing this important work to you. Having been associated with Rich Davis these past few months, I find our ideas mutually compatible. In fact, I love his ideas so much I sometimes feel as if they were my own.

You may wonder what an old printer and philosopher, dead these two hundred years, is doing back from the grave as the world approaches the

The Magic of Talk with Ben Franklin

21st century. I have come back with the expressed purpose of promoting vital ideas in self-improvement. Specifically, I have returned to correct some false or misleading statements I made back in the 18th century.

One of my primary aims in life was to help the common man learn and prosper. Though Rich Davis has a long way to go before he attains my breadth of knowledge and lofty stature, I feel he is on the same path I chose. Read this book and follow these principals if you dare to improve yourself in a most magnificent way. Remember, *How few there are who have courage enough to own their Faults, or resolution enough to mend them!*

B. Franklin

Introduction

You will quickly notice that I, Rich Davis, am not the voice narrating the first chapters of this book. Having lately encountered this eccentric old gentleman who claimed to be Benjamin Franklin in a pub in Salem, Massachusetts, I figured I would humor him by listening to his bizarre tales. The more he talked, the more fascinated I became. At length I decided maybe he *was* Mr. Franklin and I began to record the amazing information and stories he told.

The book that you have in your hands contains the words of Ben Franklin come back from the

The Magic of Talk with Ben Franklin

grave after two hundred years. You can choose to believe this or not, that's entirely up to you. Whether or not the guy is bogus, somehow his message strikes me as remarkably sane and true.

As a college teacher of oral communication, I was fascinated with Ben's description of the Talk Pyramid. I perceived how a five-week plan might be devised to assist people in perfecting skills Ben outlined in his pyramid. Together, Ben and I developed a complete program that we feel will help almost anyone achieve a happier and more successful life.

We believe in our bones that ultimately what matters in life is how we communicate with our fellow man. You'll come to find that this book is about making money, winning love, finding friendships and solving problems. It's about getting a job, getting a promotion, buying a car and selling a car. It's about the single most important human skill on the planet: talking. I am convinced the Magic of Talk can transform a mouse into a lion, a car salesman into a Lee Iacocca.

Rich Davis

1

The Miracle of Madeira

First, let me say I am glad to be among the living again. Actually, where I've been these two hundred years was not a bad place, and I was able to accomplish many useful things there; but the world is where I longed to be. Amazingly, I am the first human being ever to pass away and then come back to life an extended period of time later.   Well, this is not entirely the truth.

Let me tell you how I have managed to return. I am certain you will not believe a word I say (and I have some very important things to tell you) until I

The Magic of Talk with Ben Franklin

convince you that I am in fact Ben Franklin come back to the world of the living.

Around the year 1760, I had occasion to visit a friend of mine where I was residing in London, England. We were sitting in his library discussing the latest Indian uprising in the Colonies, as I recall, when a servant brought to my friend a package lately arrived from Virginia. To our considerable delight, the package contained, among other things, several bottles of Madeira wine. Without a moment's hesitation, my friend called for glasses and poured us both a generous portion.

Just as I was about to take the first sip from my glass, I noticed three flies, obviously drowned, floating on the top of the wine in my glass. I recalled to my friend an experiment I had read about regarding reviving drowned flies by setting them out in the sun. We immediately decided, somewhat skeptically, to try this experiment with our Virginia flies.

We set the flies on a cloth in the afternoon sun and waited. Precisely two hours later, two of the flies began to stir about. They moved their hindmost legs, wiped their eyes with their front legs, and then sailed off into the London sky. By nightfall the third fly had shown no signs of revival so we threw him out.

Thirty years passed. It was 1790, I was eighty-four years old and dying. For several years I had

The Miracle of Madeira

suffered grievously from gout, and I was physically ready to move on to another plane. Mentally, I was still sharp and active as ever. In April of that year, I began to fail rapidly. I knew it was only a matter of days before I would depart this earth, and not being an overly religious person and not looking forward to the realm I might be visiting next, my mind began to deal with the problem.

On April 16th a possible solution came to me. The flies. Madeira wine. Why not?

I called together a group of my young friends (at eighty-four everyone is young but you) and I requested them to build a large cask and fill it to the brim with Madeira wine, save the last two or three inches. One of my friends from Massachusetts agreed to store the cask in his wine cellar, his house being near my hometown of Boston.

The next day Ben Franklin died, supposedly. Actually, my friends interred my living body in the cask of Madeira wine and the funeral, which I have learned twenty thousand attended, entailed the burial of an empty coffin.

I recall quite clearly my friends hoisting me up and then lowering me down into the wine cask. The coolness of the wine rapidly soothed my aching body. The fumes of the wine and an occasional taste of the remarkable beverage relaxed my mind and

The Magic of Talk with Ben Franklin

sent me slowly but steadily toward a state of mental abeyance. Sometime later I lost consciousness which I was not to recover for over two hundred years.

Two months ago, workers tearing down a house in Salem, Massachusetts, to make way for what you call an interstate highway being built there, discovered an old, very large wine cask in the basement. The men carried the cask up the stairs, rolled it out on the front lawn, and attacked it with sledgehammers. With a great sigh the old cask suddenly burst open and much to everyone's surprise, out rolled Ben Franklin!

Having a deadline to meet and not knowing exactly what to do with an obviously dead body, the workers left my corpse out on the front lawn and went back to their business of tearing down the house. Several hours later, the noon-time sun having a chance to work its magic on my bloated and wine-logged body, I began to gradually regain my senses. When I opened my eyes, I saw the destruction of the house in progress and I heard the raucous noise of the workers. I understood immediately what had happened, and I decided to get away from that place as quickly as possible. Amazingly, no one saw me pick myself up, smooth out my clothing, and amble off.

The Miracle of Madeira

That's how I came to cheat the grim reaper. I must say, I have come back to the world of the living in remarkable condition. Apparently the aging wine worked somehow to make my old body *younger*. There is no trace of my old friend Gout, and the pain I suffered with years has entirely vanished.

I suggested earlier that coming back to life was not entirely a truthful way to describe what I did. Yes, I was unconscious. No, I was not dead.

I was suspended in a world between life and death, not quite awake but not entirely insensible, either. It was like being asleep for two hundred years.

While suspended in this somnolent state these past two centuries, many many thoughts and images coursed through my mind. Most had to do with daily events of my life: I remembered hawking the *The New-England Courant* through the streets of Boston; I vividly saw myself swimming the three and one-half miles from Chelsea to Blackfryars on the Thames; I felt the soft touch of my dear Mme. Brillon.

But much work passed through my vision, also. I composed and typeset many pages of *The Pennsylvania Gazette* and *Poor Richard's Almanack*. I performed many experiments of a scientific nature; for example, I determined how to make electricity light a lamp and power a mill. I balanced my account books and conducted negotiations of business and politics.

Finally, and most importantly, I indulged my passion for self-improvement. In my dreams for two hundred years, I reviewed the plans and projects I had developed for my own improvement, most notably the scheme I had for attaining moral perfection. I also considered the voluminous advice I offered others for improving themselves, which appeared in *Poor Richard's*, my *Autobiography*, and the thousands of letters I wrote. In comparing my life with the advice I gave others, there seemed to be a discrepancy between what I advised people to do to achieve success and how I actually did it.

I must say it sorely worried me that I left something of great importance out of my messages to people about how to find happiness and success in the world. Now that I've been given a second chance to walk this great, green planet I am determined to correct the record.

2

The Magic of Talk Pyramid

It was not long after I entered the dream-state that a curious image began asserting itself in my mind. At first I thought the figure to be an isosceles triangle, part of some mathematical exercise or puzzle. Then I recognized it for what it was, a pyramid. Now, I had heard of the ancient pyramids and the various mysteries associated with them. I wondered what this image was doing in my mind.

Gradually, over many years, the truth became known. First, lines dividing the pyramid into equal parts became apparent. Then the words Self, One-to-One, In Groups, and Before Groups appeared. Finally, the key that made the whole intelligible to me came into view: Talk Pyramid.

Talk Pyramid

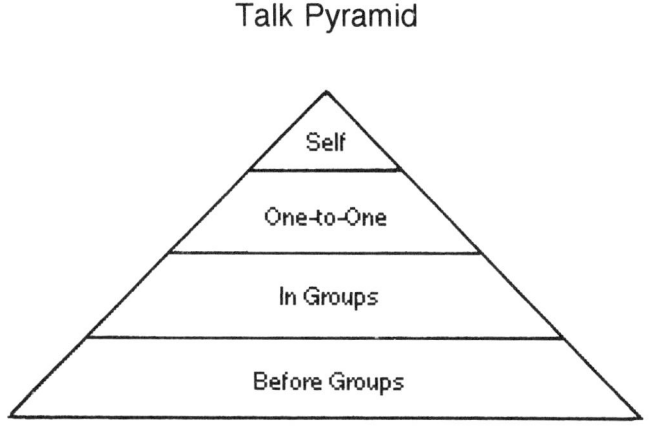

The Talk Pyramid is a graphic representation of what I believe to be the road to happiness and success in life. Each section of the pyramid stands for one of four types of personal communication in which everyone should attempt to excel. Improving skills in any one of these areas will make a person's life better in a multitude of ways. Excellence in all areas will bring untold rewards of happiness and success hardly imaginable by the average man or woman. The fact is people of ordinary talents and abilities can make themselves extraordinary by developing a few simple habits of enjoyable, effective,

The Magic of Talk Pyramid

exciting personal communication.

I looked at the Talk Pyramid and understood immediately how I succeeded in life. From the early days of my reckless youth till the last day of my wizened old age, I was a wonderful talker. I talked in exciting, positive ways to myself, individuals I encountered during the course of a day, among groups of associates, and before audiences large and small. This I realized was what differenced me from the common run of man. I got along with most folks extremely well, and they rewarded me with their friendship, their business, their ideas, and sometimes their love.

At this time you may be wondering just how you can develop wonderful talking skills. Well, Rich Davis and I have put together a Five-Week Plan that makes learning as easy as turning on a machine and opening your ears. All you will have to do is record five magical messages and listen to them occasionally. After having tried this myself, I say it couldn't be simpler! Marvelous invention, the tape recorder.

A word of caution before you get started: You likely won't achieve final perfection of the four skill areas in five weeks, but if you follow our instructions you should see a marked improvement during this time period. You can repeat the Five-Week Plan whenever you like, and your skills will improve each

The Magic of Talk with Ben Franklin

time you do. Education and change are lifetime programs, so don't try to rush the process. Poor Richard said, *What one relishes, nourishes.* Plan to have fun and take your gains where you find them. You may be astounded at what happens.

The plan of this book is for me to first discuss the Talk Pyramid. Then Rich Davis will take you through the Five-Week Plan. Follow this program step-by-step and you will soon learn why we call it The Magic of Talk.

3

Self-Communication

Each of us continually talks to ourselves as we go through every day, and what we say usually determines whether we will be successful at what we are doing or not. Think about that for a minute.

Imagine you are going to speak to an interview committee about being hired for a position. As you are preparing for this meeting the thoughts go through your mind: "They probably won't want me"; "I'm too young, old, tall, short, fat, skinny for the job"; "They will probably want someone with more experience." If those are the types of thoughts you are having going into the interview, how do you think you will do when you are seated face-to-face with the committee? On the other hand, if you are thinking to yourself: "I'm perfect for this position," "I can do this job better than anyone else in the world," "I am a talented, industrious employee who will make them glad they hired me," what will be your attitude at the interview?

The fact is a great many people continually abuse themselves in their self-talk. Every time they make a mistake or things just don't turn out right, they begin fussing at themselves. They say things like "You're an idiot. You can't do anything right." Even when things go well they say, "It was luck. Next time you'll botch it up good." I once wrote: *Is there anything men take more pains about than to make themselves unhappy?* You'll find that calling yourself an idiot creates pain; forgiving yourself and laughing at your mistakes eases the pain and makes you happier.

I must say I was a good self-communicator. My whole life I thought highly of myself, and I suppose some people thought this a defect. When I told my friends about my plan for attaining moral perfection through the attainment of twelve virtues, one well-meaning soul suggested I add a thirteenth– humility!

Self-Communication

Excess pride and vaingloriousness can be as harmful as too little, but these days and times I find most folks lack self-esteem rather than possess too much. In fact, I doubt if you *can* think too highly of yourself. Of course, you don't want your pride to show in a disagreeable way to others.

The obvious question now becomes, "How can you improve self-communication?"

One good way is to listen to the words you speak to yourself. *Get into the habit of not speaking to yourself negatively at all!* Then, attempt to insert positive thoughts into your head as much as possible. Do this simply by reading, thinking, or listening to things that make you feel good.

Believe it or not there is something good that comes from every action on earth. Next time you have a bit of bad luck, or even a major disaster, reflect upon what is good about the situation. You will find worry, tension, anger and sadness disappear when you confront a negative situation with positive thoughts.

Another way to improve your self-communication is to infuse your brain with uplifting thoughts and mental pictures. Rich Davis has written a series of meditations that are meant to teach communication skills, while improving self-esteem and confidence. By continually reading these messages (or listening to them on a tape recorder), you can fill your head with positive, wonderful thoughts that will help you tremendously in your daily life. These messages are the heart of the Five-Week Plan, which will be discussed later.

There are many other ways you can work on your self-communication, most of which have been used by man in one way or another since long before my time: meditation, visualization, prayer, affirmation. I believe *anything* you do to eliminate negative thoughts and add positive ones will benefit you.

4

One-to-One Talk: Making People Talk

Lately, I have been reading what historians have had to say about me these two hundred years I've been away:

> Franklin's services as a diplomat in France helped greatly in winning the Revolutionary War. Many historians consider him the ablest and most successful diplomat that America has ever sent abroad.

The Magic of Talk with Ben Franklin

Born poor in colonial Boston, he was at ease in Quaker Philadelphia, in royal London, and in elegant Paris; as much at home in St. Andrews as in Passy, or on the Pennsylvania wilderness frontier.

He was father of all the Yankees. His worldly wisdom was suited to the philosophers in Paris and Edinburgh; it was suited too to the old wives in the chimney corner, summing up a lifetime of neighborly experience.

To many Americans, Benjamin Franklin is the epitome of all that America should be, the patriot as responsible as Washington for prizing the young Colonies from the grip of the British, the successful businessman as well as that rare bird, the honest politician.

Very kind words. You wonder how I was able to rise from poverty, start a newspaper, write and publish a best-selling almanac, engage in countless community service projects, conduct numerous scientific experiments that made me world famous, and help secure the independence of my country? Let me tell you I did it primarily by making people talk to me. I was, and am, a very convivial person, and most of my business was conducted through other people.

One-to-One Talk: Making People Talk

I helped them. They helped me. As Poor Richard said, *A true Friend is the best Possession.*

So, you want to know how I got people to talk to me? I explain the method quite clearly in the early pages of my *Autobiography*. I asked questions. I acted the "humble inquirer," a technique I borrowed from Socrates. Thomas Jefferson, a fine young man I am glad to see became the third president of this country, took note of my conversational habits. He reportedly said: "If he [Ben Franklin] was urged to announce an opinion, he did it rather by asking questions, as if for information . . . . "

There are of course many other ways to get people to talk to you. As Rich Davis says in his meditations, you can ask for advice, give a compliment, make a startling statement, smile and be friendly. The best way to make people talk is to encourage them to talk about things of interest to them. Being an exceptional listener, making the person talking to you feel he or she has your complete attention and interest, is one of the kindest things you can do for others.

To develop the habit of making people talk, simply take the time to do it daily. Develop a sincere and hearty interest in other people, and show that you care by being a wonderful listener. After a few days you'll find that your interest and focus on other people is more easy and natural. After a fortnight you should find that making people talk is something you do habitually, like getting dressed in the morning or saying your prayers. But a lot more fun!

5

One-to-One Talk: Improving Your Talk

Possibly eighty percent of good talking is good listening and encouraging others to talk. However, when it is your turn to speak it is helpful if you have something to say!

In most conversations I had no problem finding something to say because my mind was always focused outward. I was interested in *everything*, and I found that the more I talked the more I learned and the more I had to say for future conversations. What happens with many people who have problems talking with others is that they are focused inward.

They are thinking continually about themselves, what they will say and do, and how people will perceive them.

A good way to overcome the bad habit of looking inward is to learn how to read other people. Develop the positive habit of observing the facial features and body language of others, and attempt to discover how they are feeling and what they are thinking about. You will likely find that two weeks of practice will make you quite proficient in this activity. It is not necessary that you understand completely what is happening in other people's minds. The goal is to pay attention to them and obtain a general impression of their mental and emotional states.

As you learn to read people you will soon come to understand the power your words and actions have to change the moods and thoughts of others. Next time you encounter a person who is unhappy or disturbed, aim through a word or act to alter his or her mood for the better. When you see a big smile replace the frown you will understand again why talk is magic. That reminds me of one of my sayings from Poor Richard's, *Tart Words make no Friends: a spoonful of honey will catch more flies than a Gallon of Vinegar.*

I would be remiss if I were to overlook another aspect of improving your talk: acquiring interesting

One-to-One Talk: Improving Your Talk

things to talk about. You will find that the more you talk to interesting, informed people the more you have to talk about. This is because good conversation is instructive. Many wise people have obtained *all* of their knowledge orally. I am a great advocate of reading, but nothing enhances learning quite so much as talking about what you have read, studied, or heard.

One way to acquire interesting things to say is to collect, store and use daily quotations, jokes, bon mots, poems, epigrams, facts, anecdotes, news items, and anything else that happens to suit your interest and style of conversation. All my life I received great joy and instruction from clever quotations and sayings, "gleanings" I called them. These gleanings I put into *Poor Richard's*, after rephrasing most of them to suit the tastes of my readers–and they made me a famous man at home and in Europe. You can collect your own gleanings to brighten your conversation.

Some people have the mistaken idea that they have to be an expert in a field to talk about it. What you know, think, believe or even suspect, you can talk about. To make your talk more authoritative you can always quote experts or mention studies (found in newspapers and magazines) that support your position. Learn to trust yourself, your mind, your knowledge, and your opinions. But always be careful not to undermine the confidence and stability of others through your talk. A good rule is to always use your talk to boost others, to make them feel good. This does not mean that you must downplay yourself or make yourself appear in a bad light.

One of the great erratum of my life regarding advice I handed down to others is found in my *Autobiography*. In chronicling the thirteen virtues I wished to obtain, I included: *Silence. Speak not but what may benefit others or yourself. Avoid trifling conversation.* I see now that if I had mastered this "virtue" I likely would never have risen above my initial status as printer's apprentice.

6

Talking in Groups

Let's see. What are a few of the major accomplishments of Benjamin Franklin?
 • I developed a successful business that allowed me to retire at age forty-two to public service and the advancement of science.
 • I conducted many important scientific experiments that eventually made me world famous.
 • I helped initiate countless community service projects including a volunteer fire department, the first subscription library in the country, the Penn-

The Magic of Talk with Ben Franklin

sylvania hospital, and an academy that became the University of Pennsylvania.

• I served as a highly successful diplomat and public servant–the only person to sign The Declaration of Independence, the Treaty of Alliance with France, the Treaty of Peace with Great Britain, and the Constitution of the United States.

I could go on and on–but why? The fact is I accomplished a lot in my eighty-four years on earth, and almost everything I did was done working in groups of people. I was a great joiner, a great organizer for action. I belonged to a number of groups, clubs, and organizations, many of which I started or helped found.

One writer kindly wrote about my efforts during the Revolutionary War: *Peace negotiations reached success only because throughout his years in Paris, Franklin had remained in touch with a number of his British friends and cronies . . . .*

Actually, the same could be said of all of my successes. I succeeded because I talked to others and helped them succeed. And usually, my work and socializing was done within groups of people.

So, you ask, what's Ben Franklin's secret to communicating well with people in groups?

First, use many of the skills you use in talking to people one-to-one. Get out of yourself and into

Talking in Groups

other folks. Learn to read people. Brighten up your conversation.

Second, schedule and attend events frequently that allow you to interact with others in groups. There is no substitute for actually putting yourself on the line, being there. The more you do something, the easier and more familiar it becomes. Most people who have difficulty interacting with others do so for the simple reason they don't do it often enough.

There are a number of specific tips for socializing in groups that Rich will cover in his meditation on the subject. The message I would like to leave you with is simply this: You are important. Your opinions are important. You deserve to be heard. Don't let a feeling of discomfort keep you from mixing and mingling with the beautiful variety of folks that make up this planet. If you keep your focus outward, you will find richness and magic in your group meetings.

Rich Davis shared with me the jolly but sage advice of somebody named Mel Brooks:

If you're alive, you got to flap your arms and legs, you got to jump around a lot, you got to make a lot of noise, because life is the very opposite of death. And therefore, as I see it, if you're quiet, you're not living. You've got to be noisy, or at least your thoughts should be noisy and colorful and lively.

*Human felicity is produced
not so much by great pieces of good fortune
that seldom
happen, as by little advantages
that occur every day.*

7

Talking Before Groups

On February 13, 1766 I stood before the House of Commons in England and answered 174 questions regarding American reaction to the hated Stamp Act. If I must say so myself I was brilliant. On February 22 the Act was repealed, and I became something of a hero, both in America and abroad.

Most folks don't have to get up in front of an audience and speak. This is not an activity that comes naturally to most, and it takes a bit of practice to do it well. That's one reason I founded the Junto, or Leather Apron Club, a group of young men

The Magic of Talk with Ben Franklin

interested in self-improvement who met every Friday evening. Periodically, each member of the club was required to make a presentation before the group.

When we began the Junto in 1727 most of the members were still apprentices in their trades. I, myself, was but twenty-one years old. Through the desire for self-improvement and the willingness to form friendships that would lead to this end, many of those young men achieved prominence in the world. One man, a surveyor, became surveyor-general. Another, a merchant's clerk, became a merchant and a provincial judge.

"But why is public speaking so important?" you ask.

If you rise far in your line of business you will be called on to speak for the edification of others. It behooves you to be able to perform this function as painlessly as possible—for your sake and your audience's! It may be also that speaking before groups will play a vital role in your rise to success.

The next question you might ask is "How does a person learn how to be a good speaker?" I would say join the Junto; but, unfortunately, there aren't too many Leather Apron groups around these days. The next best thing is to join a Toastmasters club. I have attended a few Toastmasters meetings with Rich Davis in various cities, and I must say members

Talking Before Groups

receive valuable training, instruction and experience. Not only do they learn how to speak before groups, but they also develop myriad other skills that are useful in personal and professional life. These include: mixing in groups, communicating one-to-one, leadership training, speech evaluation, and much more.

Other ways to obtain public speaking skills include:

1. Join organizations and community-service groups that require you to speak before others.

2. Take a public speaking class. High school students will likely have courses, programs, or groups available that will allow them to develop speaking skills. Colleges also offer a range of courses and programs, often open to people in the community as well as students. For people interested in short-term, time-tested instruction, Rich Davis recommends Dale Carnegie courses highly.

3. Become a member of a speakers bureau for your favorite cause. Many groups will provide training so you can speak effectively before others in their behalf.

4. Do it yourself. If you have a burning desire to speak about something, you can put together your own program and take it to the public. Rich Davis has been scheduling programs in libraries and

college continuing education centers for years. You can too!

A word to the wise: don't hesitate to stand up before a group and talk. If it feels uncomfortable at first, remember what an ordeal it was to learn how to swim. And aren't you glad you did!

Poor Richard offers some sage advice that seems to apply here: *Hide not your Talents, they for Use were made: "What's a Sun-Dial in the Shade?"*

Since Rich is the public speaking expert, I will leave the specific advice in this area to him. I have read the meditation called Magical Public Speaking and give it my highest approbation.

8

The Five-Week Plan

Thanks, Ben, for your help with the first part of this book. I'll take over for a while on this magical journey of self-improvement and discovery.

When Ben first explained to me his Talk Pyramid idea, I immediately recognized its value, its brilliance. Here finally was a concept the average person could use to develop his or her personal communication skills. The "what to do" was presented in such a neat, intelligent, appealing way. However, I soon began to wonder about the "how to do" part of it. How might the Talk Pyramid be translated into an actual, step-by-step program people might be able to implement quickly and easily?

Through further discussions with Ben and research of current literature on self-improvement and personal communication, I came up with the Five-Week Plan. My goal was to develop a fool-proof method of self-improvement that would be simple, fun, and effective.

The plan I have developed, I believe, is as close to perfection as can be devised by man. (If that sounds a little vain, it's probably the influence of my new friend rubbing off on me.) The plan is good because it explains exactly what to do and requires very little effort. Most of the work is done in the subconscious mind, which reduces the need for willpower and self-discipline.

A basic premise of the plan is that you can improve your "talk" skills by listening to yourself talk. Specifically, I believe that by listening repeatedly to the right messages (recorded in your own voice) that your conscious and subconscious minds will begin to take action. Without great effort you will find yourself actually changing lifelong speaking and action habits. This is a method tested and proven by medical doctors and mental health professionals, and it is the easiest and most enjoyable way I know to

The Five-Week Plan

change behavior.

I have developed transcripts for the Five-Week Plan that cover self-communication and the other vital areas of oral communication. Unless you want to read your message (which is okay, but will require a bit more time each day), you'll need to record and play back frequently the five transcripts. The idea is to suggest to your brain changes you want to make. You should use little or no force to make yourself carry out the suggestions; but when you notice positive action as a result of the tape message, you should give yourself a reward, or at least a little appreciation.

I include a schedule for listening to the tapes in the Five-Week Plan and a "progress" sheet for recording times you've actually taken action as a result of the transcripts. The more you reward and appreciate the action you take as a result of the tapes, the more you will continue doing it.

I've also included a quiz that's useful for gauging your progress in the Five-Week Plan. The quiz, the transcripts, and the progress sheet are all you'll need to improve your talk immediately and continuously. I believe you'll find this program fun, and I know you can achieve wondrous results using it.

You'll improve your attitude and find more joy

The Magic of Talk with Ben Franklin

and excitement in the world, guaranteed!

The Five-Week Plan

THE FIVE-WEEK PLAN   WEEK ONE

1. Read *The Magic of Talk*. Pay special attention to Chapters 3 and 9.

2. Write out benefits you can expect to receive from improved communications with others. Save for future reference.

3. Take The Magic of Talk Quiz. Don't write in book so you can take the quiz over later. Record and save your scores for use later.

4. Make a recording of Week 1 transcript, Walk in Beauty. Talk in a slow, relaxed, voice. You may not like the way you sound on tape initially, but you will get used to hearing your own voice and you can work on improving it as you go. Don't expect tape to be perfect.

5. Listen to Walk in Beauty at least once each day. When you notice yourself taking action as a result of the tape's message, record the event on your progress sheet.

The Magic of Talk with Ben Franklin

THE FIVE-WEEK PLAN   WEEK TWO

1. Review *The Magic of Talk*. Pay special attention to Chapters 4 and 10.

2. Review the list of benefits you expect to receive from improved communication with others.

3. Make a recording of Week 2 transcript, Make Them Glad They Talked With You. Plan to enjoy making this recording.

4. Listen to Make Them Glad at least once each day. When you notice yourself taking action as a result of the tape's message, record the event on your progress sheet. If time permits, listen to Walk in Beauty several times this week, also.

The Five-Week Plan

THE FIVE-WEEK PLAN   WEEK THREE

1. Review briefly *The Magic of Talk*. Focus on Chapters 5 and 11.

2. Review the list of benefits you expect to receive from improved communication with others.

3. Make a recording of Week 3 transcript, Improve Your Talk. Plan to enjoy making and listening to this recording.

4. Listen to Improve Your Talk at least once each day. Record action taken on your progress sheet. If time permits, listen to Walk in Beauty and Make Them Glad a couple of times each this week, also.

The Magic of Talk with Ben Franklin

THE FIVE-WEEK PLAN   WEEK FOUR

1. Review briefly *The Magic of Talk*. Focus on Chapters 6 and 12.

2. Review your list of benefits you expect to receive from improved communication with others.

3. Make a recording of Week 4 transcript, The Magic of Mixing. Plan to enjoy making and listening to this recording.

4. Listen to The Magic of Mixing at least once each day. Record action taken on your progress sheet. If time permits, listen to earlier tapes in the series, also.

The Five-Week Plan

THE FIVE-WEEK PLAN   WEEK FIVE

1. Review briefly *The Magic of Talk*. Focus on Chapters 7 and 13.

2. Review the list of benefits you expect to receive from improved communication with others.

3. Make a recording of Week 5 transcript, Magical Public Speaking.

4. Listen to Magical Public Speaking at least once each day. Record action taken on your progress sheet. If time permits, listen to earlier tapes in the series.

5. Take the Magic of Talk Quiz. Compare score with previous score: does it reflect gains you feel you have made? Consider ways to make the program work better for you in the future.

The Magic of Talk with Ben Franklin

The Magic of Talk Quiz

Rate yourself 1-10 on the following 10 items. 100 = a perfect score. After you've completed the test, you might want to have someone else evaluate you. The average of these two scores should give you a very good idea where you stand as a talker. <u>Most scores on this test are very low, so don't be discouraged.</u>

To determine progress in Five-Week Plan, retake test after fifth week. To continue improvement, repeat Five-Week Plan and retake test again.

_____ 1. I feel I am a positive, happy, and friendly person.

_____ 2. People perceive me as being positive, enthusiastic, and outgoing.

_____ 3. I communicate in an exciting, creative, and supporting way with friends, family and associates.

_____ 4. I make it a point to meet new people and talk with them.

_____ 5. I am fully aware of the importance of being able to talk enjoyably, intelligently and creatively with others.

_____ 6. I know how to get others to talk intelligently and creatively with me and I do it frequently.

_____ 7. When I'm tired or feeling down, I am able to reclaim my energy and positive attitude before others notice.

_____ 8. I am a good "mixer" at parties or business meetings, speaking creatively and intelligently to many different people one-on-one or in small groups.

_____ 9. I don't hesitate to speak out before a large group, and I feel I communicate forcefully and intelligently when I do so.

_____ 10. At a party or business meeting, I would not hesitate to start a conversation with someone I don't know.

_____ Total Score   Name _____ Date _____

The Five-Week Plan

The Magic of Talk Progress Sheet
(sample)
Week 1

Positive actions taken as a result of listening to tape:

5/25 Thought about W. James quote and overcame anger

5/25 Listened to Tape #1 and felt energized afterwards

5/26 Said an uplifting word to send my wife on her day

The Magic of Talk with Ben Franklin

The Magic of Talk Progress Sheet

Week _____

Positive actions taken as a result of listening to tape:

_____
_____
_____
_____
_____
_____
_____
_____
_____
_____
_____
_____
_____
_____
_____
_____
_____
_____
_____
_____
_____
_____

The Five-Week Plan

A Word About the Transcripts

Transcripts are positive messages that correspond to vital areas of the Talk Pyramid. To learn and profit from these messages only two things are required, repetition and reinforcement. Read or listen to the messages on tape as frequently as possible, and reward yourself (mentally or otherwise) when you find yourself taking action as a result of the messages.

Think of the transcript message as suggestions, not things you *must* do. Force is not required and may prove detrimental to your progress. Have fun with your tapes (or reading), and feel free to alter the transcripts and the Five-Week Plan to suit your own needs or desires.

I have found a key ingredient to successfully initiating a change of behavior is perceiving the new activity as a pleasurable one. Trust me, making and listening to tapes can be fun!

Tape-Making Tips

Use whatever tape recorder you have available and you like. I use a cassette "boom box" for my recording and have different players located where I listen to the tapes: bedroom, bathroom, car.

Eliminate or reduce all possible distractions and interruptions when making a tape. When actually taping, don't worry about minor imperfections such as occasional mispronunciations or background noise. The less you think about these, the less they will matter. Future tapes will be much better than the first ones you make.

Use background "mood" music to make tapes sound more professional. I record a few sentences with the music first to be sure the volume is right.

Experiment with your voice to find a tone that sounds best on tape. This has been a wonderful bonus of the program for me because I find I have actually changed my speaking voice for the better as a result.

Week One

9

Walk in Beauty

I picture myself in a special, relaxing, enjoyable place. This is my mental sanctuary, a place where I leave all my daily cares and worries behind. In this place I am invincible. Totally relaxed, confident, serene. I see the place right now. I see myself relaxing comfortably there.

I reflect on my life. I realize I have more energy and vigor than ever before. This is because I take good care of my body, mind and soul.

The Magic of Talk with Ben Franklin

I eat sanely and lightly foods that rejuvenate my mind and body, not make me feel tired and sluggish. Ben Franklin said, "Eat to live, and not live to eat." He also said, "Eat not to dullness; drink not to elevation." I don't!

I sleep soundly and as long as necessary to totally rest my mind and body. I know how much sleep I need, and I make sure I get it. Sometimes, if it helps to boost my energy level, I rest or take a short nap during the day.

The main reason I have so much energy, though, is because I have a strong, vibrant, new-found enthusiasm for life. I have learned that absolutely nothing counts except what I get done today–and so I make sure I get maximum happiness and productivity out of each day.

I truly believe the following statement by Thomas Dreier: "If we are ever to enjoy life, now is the time– not tomorrow, nor next year, nor in some future life after we have died. The best preparation for a better life next year is a full, complete, harmonious, joyous life this year. Our beliefs in a rich future life are of little importance unless we coin them into a rich present life. Today should always be our most wonderful day."

Because I don't worry about the past or future I can go all out today. I can put a hundred percent of my focus and energy into the task at hand, whether it be a major business decision or fifteen minute walk through a city park. I put energy and enthusiasm into everything I do. I feel vibrant. I act vibrant. I am vibrant. And everyone around me smiles and tingles because of my zest for life.

I love every day because every day I plan and do important tasks. I enjoy setting a course and then following it. I also love being spontaneous and turning things upside down once in a while. I love my life and all the big and little pleasures I can cram into a day. As Nietzsche said, "When one has much to put into them, a day has a hundred pockets." My days *all* have a hundred pockets!

I am a physical being, and I love to put my body in motion. I'm fit because I eat moderately and exercise frequently. I don't have to count calories, fat grams or worry about cholesterol. I don't have to force myself to exercise. I eat foods that are good for me in moderate amounts, and I exercise because I love to. I don't worry, I simply eat and exercise for the good of my body and mind. The workouts I do are very enjoyable and relaxing. I've found the perfect exercise for me and I do it frequently, out of joy.

I am a mental being. I love to put my brain to work. I challenge my mind by reading, by thinking, by taking courses, by talking to intelligent people. I do things I enjoy doing that work, develop, and exercise my mind. I know that most people use only a tiny portion of their brains; my goal is to use as much of mine as I possibly can. Again, I do this out of joy because it feels good. I do absolutely nothing out of fear or self-compulsion. I am very careful not to exert force upon myself to do things I hate *or* love to do. I select things to do because they give me pleasure, either in doing them or getting them done.

I am a spiritual being. I realize that most of what I am is not apparent to the eye or consciously understandable. I have a wonderful inner existence that I seek to explore every day. In many ways it is like venturing into an unknown wilderness; in other ways it's like getting in touch with a friend from my childhood after many years. The spiritual being inside of me is familiar yet strange. When I visit the inner world and get in touch with the essential me through contemplation or meditation, I renew my energy, vigor and strength of purpose. I draw wisdom from the inner me and from the powerful divine source with which it is in direct contact. To explore this inner world and to commune with the inner me, I know all I have to do is shut out the world and all its distractions for half an hour and still my mind.

I am the most positive, confident person in the world. Every day I set out with a mental picture of what I want my day to be. I see great work being done. I see me engaged in savoring the multitude of free joys around me. I stop and smell the roses. I enjoy tiny wild flowers blooming in vacant lots, forest paths, or fields. I appreciate and savor all the lovely sights, sounds, smells, and sensations I experience each day. I don't postpone work, exercise, pleasure, or any vital part of my life. I do it all today with relish.

I focus on the task at hand always. Whatever I do, I do it with all my might and energy–then I go to the next thing. I don't worry, fret, or hurry. I just do the thing that I want to do, now!

I keep my brain loaded with positive thoughts. I think positive thoughts. I read positive thoughts. I dream positive thoughts. I listen to positive thoughts on tape. I realize that positive thoughts and information

The Magic of Talk with Ben Franklin

flowing into my brain revitalizes me. William James said, "Tell him to live by yes and no–yes to everything good, no to everything bad." That's what I do. This is where my great energy, vitality and attitude come from.

I have a wonderful, new policy in my life: no negatives! I don't see problems, I see opportunities. I don't feel worry or fear, I embrace challenge. I love myself vitally and know that negative thoughts weaken and debilitate. I won't have them. I am a fine, bold, happy, strong person. There is no room in my mind or soul for a single dark thought.

I have learned that I can control my thoughts. Viktor Frankl said, the last of the human freedoms "is the ability to choose one's own attitude in any given set of circumstances, to choose one's own way." Since Frankl saw people control their thoughts and attitudes in Nazi death camps, I know I can control mine in my daily life.

Norman Vincent Peale says, "change your thoughts and you change your world." Well, I'm doing it. I see the truth in these words every day. Each day I feel my great positive outlook growing. Chuck Norris says, "a winner thinks about winning while a loser thinks about losing." I aim my thoughts always toward winning!

Every day I am confronted with hundreds of decisions–from when to climb out of bed in the morning, to what to do every moment of the day, to when to climb into bed at night. Obviously, some decisions are tougher than others, but I welcome all decisions, just the same. I enjoy making decisions. I positively thrill at saying, "Yes, I will do this," or "No, I won't do that." Each decision I make confirms the command I have over my own mind, body, and emotions. I am in charge.

Strength of character comes from decision making. I've gotten into the habit of making decisions and taking action quickly. I find movement is almost always better than hesitation. Procrastination and worry are two evils I have banished from my life forever.

I make good decisions. If the decision to be made is a large or important one, I gather all the information I need first. I think logically. I consult others who can shed light on the problem. But I always make my own decisions and I never blame another for mistakes I may make. I am not perfect and I will make mistakes. Life really would not be much fun if everything always turned out perfectly.

If the decision is not large or important, I make it quickly and move to the next thing. Yes, I enjoy making decisions. I've developed the habit of daily making good decisions as quickly as possible. I operate with strength and authority. I love my new power and confidence.

I go through my day in a friendly, outgoing way. Never in my life have I been so confident of myself or interested in other people. I smile a lot. I am very friendly. People like me and talk to me in the same friendly and creative way that I talk to them.

I don't worry about what I'm going to say or how I'm going to act around others. My focus is always on the other person's needs and interests. I am the world's greatest listener because I care about other people and really am interested in what they have to say. I take pride in my ability to make people talk–to ask the right questions, to make the right comments. I've found that every person I meet has something truly useful or interesting to offer in conversation. Often their words actually become valuable to me. I may acquire valuable knowledge or possessions through talk, though that is never my aim. My aim is always to enjoy people, to relate to them, to savor the highest pleasure on this planet–human contact.

Yes, I'm now a committed extrovert, talking in an enjoyable, creative way with many people during the course of a day. Because I enjoy the talk I find myself looking for opportunities to do it every-where I go. I don't fear speaking out in groups, mixing with people at parties, or speaking before large audiences. At this point in my life I am a trained communicator, more so than anyone else I know. I know how to talk. I enjoy talking. I do it very well.

My mission on this planet is to live each day to the best of my ability in a high state of joy. I take pleasure from every facet of my life, and I am not content to postpone my happiness even for one day. I know that the source of all happiness is my mind, so I simply make it a point to be happy all the time. Lincoln said: "Most folks are about as happy as they make up their minds to be." I believe it. I've made up my mind to be very happy.

I have a deep appreciation of the wonderful gifts I have in my life. I'm a millionaire many times over if I add up the worth of my assets. My hands, my legs, my eyes–how much are they worth? The mountains, the sea, the sun, the moon are mine–what would I take for them? My family, my friends, the wonderful potential of future human relationships–can I put a price tag on these?

The fact is if I just use and enjoy the things I have that cannot be purchased, I am richer by far than the millionaire who spends his time counting his money and collecting things.

So many people, as Thoreau said, lead lives of quiet desperation. I live my life in noisy exhilaration. I appreciate all the things I have and take the time daily to savor them. I use my arms, legs, eyesight and other senses enjoyably, almost ecstatically. Each day I wallow in simple pleasures: sunsets, snow fights, fresh air that goes deep into the lungs, sensuous stretches.

Life is truly a movable feast, and I eat it up voraciously every day.

I am glad I have this transcript and have discovered this way to prepare myself for wonderful, vibrant living. I understand the simple method behind Magic of Talk transcripts: suggestion and repetition of vital, positive thoughts. By hearing these sane and true thoughts over and over, I gradually begin to implement them into my life. They become part of my thinking and action patterns. The idea in its simplest form is to replace negative, destructive ideas and thoughts with vital, positive, constructive ones. Right now my head is filled to the brim with wonderful, exciting thoughts that are already working to generate energy, confidence, enthusiasm and excitement in my life.

I believe in the method behind these transcripts. I know they will work as long as I use them with faith and acceptance. In my life at this time there is no room anywhere for doubt or uncertainty. I am taking a wild and wonderful leap of faith, and I see it pay off every day in a great new attitude and way of life.

The Navajo Indians have a most exciting concept of life. They believe that every person should Walk in Beauty; and if something should occur to disturb this mental balance, they have elaborate ceremonies to restore the balance.

My overall objective in life is to each day Walk in Beauty. All the elements in my life are blended together to create a kind of living art, a kind of life perfection. I know inconsistencies happen and I know I won't always make the right decision, take the right action, or succeed at everything I attempt. But I plan to always keep moving in a positive direction, keep affirming my love for myself and everyone else, and to always, without hesitation or doubt, Walk in Beauty.

Week Two

10

Make Them Glad They Talked with You

I am in my sanctuary, a relaxing, comfortable place. A place I can be myself. A place where I am all powerful. A place where I am confident, full of energy and vigor.

I see myself vitally interested in and caring about other people. I have learned the greatest human relations principal in the world: how to climb out of myself and into other people. I find it extremely rewarding and enjoyable to do this. For the first time in my life I feel incredibly free and easy in the presence of others; after all, I've taken the focus off me and placed it on them. I feel I am not on the spot any more. My job is to get them to talk, to perform somehow.

I care about people because other people are very interesting. I never knew how interesting they were until I started really listening to and observing them. Now I know that most other people feel and experience the same uncertainties and insecurities I've had. I see my job now is to help relieve people of these negative thoughts and emotions by communicating with them freely, easily, and creatively. I know I have the power in me to bring sunshine to a cloudy face. My smile will get a smile in return. My laugh will get a laugh. My compliment will make the crabbiest person beam. I love observing in a detached way the effect my words have on others.

I picture myself now going through my day. All day long my head is full of positive, happy thoughts. My new policy is no negative thoughts ever. I must say this concept strengthens me and makes my life a whole lot more fun.

As I go through my day, I make it a point to smile,

Make Them Glad They Talked with You

speak, and be friendly to every person I meet. I love turning my happy beams of light on people. I love leaving people happier than when I found them. My aim is to always make people glad they talked with me, whether it's a big business deal or a stranger I pass on the street. I speak freely and easily to everyone, and they respond in kind to me.

I hear my voice, a voice I've decided I like. It's pleasant to the ear because I've practiced speaking into the tape recorder and reading aloud. I see my voice as being a wonderful musical instrument, one with just a little practice I can learn to play well. I don't worry about improving my voice, I simply enjoy and appreciate it.

I move through my day with strength and vigor. By focusing on others and not myself, I find that communication is much easier and more exciting. I do not have to think or worry about what I'm doing at all—my goal is simply to read others and encourage them to talk. I've found this to be the easiest thing in the world to do. All I have to do to get people to talk is ask them a question, give them a compliment, make a startling statement, or ask for advice.

People love to talk about things they know about.

The Magic of Talk with Ben Franklin

Since most folks aren't trained in personal communication, they don't have the knowledge or experience I have in this area. This means I am the communications authority in most conversations. I take pride in this knowledge and skill, and I use my abilities wisely and enjoyably.

My goal is not to take advantage of or to use people; my goal is to brighten their lives, give them a golden moment of joy. And all I have to do to accomplish this is to encourage them to talk about something that interests them.

I do not have to be a perfect human being or the greatest talker in the world. I find I've become a very good facilitator of talk, and my primary skill is the ability to make others talk. I do believe this may be the most important skill anyone can possess. And I hone this skill by doing it daily.

People see me as being friendly, outgoing, and gregarious. I do love all people; I'm fascinated by them. I mix freely and easily with others, making comments and asking questions that encourage them to talk. My talk is intelligent and creative, but I've found I don't have to be a superstar talker to make great conversation. Like Ben Franklin, I can achieve much by striving to be a "humble inquirer." My skill as a listener, as a person who can make others talk, is my greatest human relations technique.

The following are ways I have of starting conversations and keeping them going:

<u>I ask questions people will want to answer</u>. My goal is not to snoop or make a pest of myself but to get them to talk. I know I have dozens of subjects I'd like people to ask me about; my job is always to discover what *they* want to talk about. When I ask the right question and a person's face lights up with pleasure, I know I've hit my target. I bring joy into the lives of others by allowing them to talk about themselves and their interests. This is one of the nicest things I can do for others, and it helps me win friends and tons of good will.

<u>I give compliments</u>. I seek out the good, the interesting in others; and I provide honest and sincere recognition. I don't flatter, I observe and comment. I take every opportunity to put a smile on another's face through my words and deeds. I sincerely care about every single person in the world, and whatever I can do in a moment to cheer someone up, I do. I find it's easy to keep my positive attitude when I'm

making people all around me smile, laugh, and be happy.

<u>I make startling statements</u>. I've discovered by observing people react to my talk that it usually doesn't matter what I say to open a conversation, as long as I say *something*. However, I've also found that I like startling people just a bit, demonstrating my creativity by saying things just a bit out of the ordinary. Everybody says, How's it going? How are you doing? What's happening? I like to encourage people to really hear me and look at me by saying something like, "It's a great day to be alive," or "Can you tell me where a really tall building is, I want to throw myself off," or "I like that blouse, it reminds me of walking through a field of wildflowers on a spring day."

Whatever the situation and whoever I'm talking to, I know there is always a startling statement I can make to pleasingly get their attention.

I hone my ability to get people to talk by experimenting with folks in stores, supermarkets, lines at banks–wherever I happen to be. I enjoy brightening the day of customer service representatives, grocery checkout persons, and even telemarketing callers. I don't have to buy from salespersons to make them feel good. I always follow the Golden Rule: Do Unto Others As You Would Have Them Do Unto You.

By experimenting with startling statements and other dynamic methods of making people talk in fail-safe situations such as stores, I find it's easy to perfect skills that can be used in more demanding situations.

<u>I smile and am friendly to every person I meet</u>. I know that what I give is what I get, so I give smiles, compliments, and good cheer. A famous businessman once said, "I have yet to find the man . . . who did not do better work and put forth greater effort under a spirit of approval than he would ever do under a spirit of criticism."

It's a fundamental principal of human nature to desire acceptance and approval. William James said, "The deepest principle in human nature is the craving to be appreciated." I smile at people. I comment favorably about things having to do with them. I am interested in and want to talk about what interests them. Because I care about all people and bare no ill feelings for anyone (even folks who seem bent on hurting me), I find my life flows more smoothly, is filled with happy, pleasant thoughts and moments. As my animosity towards others completely disappears and I give everyone sincere appreciation, they in turn develop thoughts and actions of good will toward me.

My motto is *make a friend today.* Joseph Addison said, "Friendship improves happiness and abates misery by doubling our joy, and dividing our grief." How true. I love and cherish all the people who are close to me as my most prized possessions in life. Family, relations, friends are indeed the spice of life.

<u>I take the time to ask for advice</u>. I have learned how to win support and good will by asking people's advice about topics they will want to talk about.

Barry Farber says, "Asking for 'advice' is a fascinating tactic; some say a secret weapon." Yes, it is a secret weapon, one I use frequently to win friends, gain information and make people talk. I do not hesitate to become humble and allow others to assume a strong stance on their favorite topics. Emerson said, "Every man I meet is my superior in some way. In that, I learn of him." Not only can their words be enormously valuable to me, but in making them talk in this way, I've given them an indirect compliment and likely won a supporter.

Make Them Glad They Talked with You

So, I go through my day happy, positive and friendly, talking creatively and easily to everyone I meet. My face is friendly and smiling; my mind is alert and confident; and my talk is lively and entertaining.

I make people feel good about themselves because I encourage them to talk about things of interest to them. My ultimate goal in every contact is simply to make them glad they talked with me.

❑❑

Some inspiring affirmations that will help me improve my talk are:

I see myself smiling at people and speaking to them freely and easily.

I truly like people and I enjoy talking to them about things that interest them.

Through my talk I am able to brighten people's lives and make them feel better about themselves.

I have many friends because I make people feel special by being a great listener.

I remember people's names because I make it a

point to use their names frequently in conversations.

I am a great communicator because I genuinely care about other people.

A kind word, given sincerely and spontaneously, is one of the nicest things I do for others.

I am a "good mood" maker. My words brighten a gloomy day and change frowns to smiles and laughter.

I interact positively with all manner of people. I speak readily and people mirror my good humor, my good talk, and my enthusiasm.

❑❑

Some inspiring quotations that will help me improve my talk are:

A bit of fragrance always clings to the hand that gives you roses.
– Chinese proverb

The way to develop the best in a man is by appreciation and encouragement.
– Charles Schwab

Make Them Glad They Talked with You

Whatever kind of word thou speakest, the like shalt thou hear.
— Greek proverb

When we see men of a contrary character, we should turn inwards and examine ourselves.
— Confucius

A friend may be reckoned the masterpiece of nature.
— Ralph Waldo Emerson

Good conversation is as stimulating as black coffee, and just as hard to sleep after.
— Anne Morrow Lindbergh

Happiness is a perfume you can't pour on someone without getting some on yourself.
— Ralph Waldo Emerson

Life is to be spent, not to be saved.
— D. H. Lawrence

The great end of life is not knowledge but action.
— Thomas Huxley

I shall not pass this way again; any good, therefore, that I can do or any kindness that I can show to any

The Magic of Talk with Ben Franklin

human being, let me do it now. Let me not defer nor neglect it, for I shall not pass this way again.

— Old saying

Hope in every sphere of life is a privilege that attaches itself to action. No action, no hope.

— Peter Levi

All life is an experiment.

— Oliver Wendell Holmes, Jr.

There is no meaning to life except the meaning man gives his life by the unfolding of his powers, by living productively.

— Eric Fromm

The royal road to a person's heart is to talk about things he or she treasures most.

— Dale Carnegie

As soon as you trust yourself you will know how to live.

— Johann Wolfgang von Goethe

Life appears to me too short to be spent nursing animosity or registering wrongs.

— Charlotte Bronte

Make Them Glad They Talked with You

The first step in Making People Talk is to bring yourself to assume the awesome obligation of getting things started.

– Barry Farber

Praise is like sunlight to the warm human spirit; we cannot flower and grow without it. And yet, while most of us are only too ready to apply to others the cold wind of criticism, we are somehow reluctant to give our fellows the warm sunshine of praise.

– Dale Carnegie

Do what you can, with what you have, where you are.

– Theodore Roosevelt

Our main business is not to see what lies dimly at a distance, but to do what lies clearly at hand.

– Thomas Carlyle

Don't criticize, condemn or complain.

– Dale Carnegie

There's no single, specific secret to Making People Talk. You always know, though, when it's working. You know by the invisible light and the unmeasurable heat that descends when chitchat becomes communication. It's when eyes shine, brows furrow

The Magic of Talk with Ben Franklin

with attention and concentration. It's when everybody around, though fully dressed, seems to be sharing a hot tub. It's when time passes effortlessly as ideas crackle back and forth.

– Barry Farber

Week Three

11

Improving Your Talk

I am in my sanctuary, that special place I go to be alone with myself. I am totally at ease and comfortable. In this place I am super confident and all powerful. I am also mellow and very serene.

I reflect on my life. I focus specifically on my exciting new project, brightening my talk. I see that this project is going very well. With just a few simple actions I find I have improved my own talk five hundred percent. I would never have thought it would be so easy.

The Magic of Talk with Ben Franklin

I see myself happy and energetic, going through my day. Every encounter with people is a warm, wonderful and happy experience. Through the words I say I find I'm able to make others instantly feel good. I ask creative questions; I ask for advice; I give compliments. I speak in a lively, creative way. I notice people are always reacting positively to my words. Above all, I speak to everyone I meet in a caring, friendly manner. People feel special when I speak to them.

I am a great talker. I know more about personal communication than most other people, and I work at my "talk" every day. I do this out of joy because I have found human contact to be the most rewarding and enjoyable thing I do. Leonard Zunin said, "People are lonely because they build walls instead of windows." I tear down the walls and open windows.

The following are just a few of the ways I benefit from making great talk with others:

<u>I improve my attitude</u>. Good talk makes me feel good. I feel powerful knowing I can talk easily, fluidly and creatively with anyone. This is the most important skill I have, and it makes me feel strong and

happy to use it. Also, interrelating with others improves my positive outlook by reinforcing through action my faith in the Magic of Talk program. I continuously get warm and positive feedback from folks that my good talk is working. I notice their reactions to my talk, and I get lots of smiles, laughs, and good talk in return.

<u>I increase the number of my friends</u>. As I go through my day I take the time to let conversations and friendships develop. Because I am a lively, confident person–vitally interested in others–I find that all manner of people are attracted to me. I choose the friendships I wish to develop, and I nurture these friendships by endeavoring to spend more and better time with my friends. Benjamin Franklin said, "A true Friend is the best Possession." I believe this and seek to acquire more friends every day.

<u>I develop a network of people who can help me along the paths of personal and professional betterment</u>. I know and appreciate the fact that every human contact is exciting and valuable, but I also realize certain people can play important roles in my development, and I establish and maintain great contacts with these folks. As Harvey Mackay suggests, I seek out "Old Grizzlies" for advice and

support in matters of interest to me. These older and more experienced people help me tremendously discover paths I should take. Of course, I always make my own decisions. I also play the role of "Old Grizzly" to those younger and less experienced than I am. As a mentor I have much to offer. My skills in personal communication (and the Magic of Talk method) are just part of what I can share with others still searching for the way to go.

<u>I improve communications with loved ones</u>. I have found that thoughtful and creative talk can head off problems at home and solve others. As I share Magic of Talk ideas with loved ones, I find *their* attitudes and talk improve. When they see it work for me, they naturally begin to emulate my strategies. As I pay attention to how my words affect the moods and attitudes of family members, I adjust my talk to keep them positive, productive and happy. I am amazed how my attitudes and words affect *them*. I find a dramatic decrease in family squabbles and arguments. I find a dramatic increase in confidence, self-esteem, and creative talk in every member of the household. Suddenly we are getting along so much better. Suddenly we are getting so much more done!

I know my most important "talking" skill is listening,

Improving Your Talk

encouraging others to talk. But I find it very helpful to be a great talker, too. My free and easy manner breaks the ice and encourages others to talk. My bright and lively talk is a stimulant to others–they seek to elevate the quality of their talk when they encounter mine. Barry Farber says to add "wrinkles" to your talk. He calls a wrinkle "the conversational equivalent of the big play in baseball, football, tennis, or golf that erases hours of zombified watching from our faces and makes us say, 'Wow!'" Wrinkles can be "jokes, lines, quips, squelches, sayings, proverbs, put-downs, mottoes, aphorisms, and battle cries . . . " or anything that serves to make your talk stand out from the routine.

I have developed the habit of great, spontaneous talk. I practice on store clerks, sales people, grocery store employees and I continue with everyone else I meet. I say interesting things, and I encourage everyone I meet to talk. As I shine in talk, I do my best to help them shine. If I can encourage someone to say something bright, cheerful, witty, or intelligent, I make them feel great about themselves.

My good talk makes me feel good because I see how it enlivens others. I enjoy saying things that awaken people's brains, puts a smile on their faces. I realize most folks are bored to tears with lethargic, mundane talk. It takes very little to break the cycle of routine talk and start astounding people.

One of the most exciting and powerful habits I've developed is the ability to read other people. I know that communication goes better when I can get out of my own little internal world and focus on stimulating others with my talk. I've found that by observing others I can tell pretty much what they are thinking. I can watch their moods, emotions, and thinking patterns at work. I'm never surprised when people take bizarre or extreme actions because I've been observing their facial expressions, body language, and the tone of their voices.

It's the easiest thing in the world to read other people–all I have to do is pay attention to them. Of course, I realize many people might not like to think they are being read, so I don't advertise the fact. People do love a great listener and the fact that others are interested in them. Reading them is simply how I am able to determine what to talk about and how my talk is affecting them. Dale Carnegie said about his classic book *How to Win Friends and Influence People*: "If, as a result of reading this book, you get only one thing–an increased tendency to

Improving Your Talk

think always in terms of the other person's point of view, and see things from that person's angle as well as your own–it may easily prove to be one of the stepping-stones of your career." Obviously, being able to read people and to see things as they do is an important skill indeed.

As I observe people I'm able to say things that get their interest and alter their moods. If someone is preoccupied with a particular problem, I can channel the conversation toward constructively dealing with the problem. If someone is sad or depressed I can change the conversation to a brighter or happier topic. Through my words and actions I am able to allay fear, anger, worry and sadness. As I talk to people I watch their moods and emotions change for the better. I see my talk actually work to make them smile, laugh, change their whole attitude. This is power. This is fun!

Specific things I look for to help me read people are:

Facial expression. Are they smiling, frowning, pensive? Do their eyes and mouth show worry, fear, uncertainty? I know instantly how another person is feeling simply by looking at his or her face.

Posture. Are they positively, vibrantly physically animated? Or, are they slumped over, looking like a homeless puppy?

Gestures. People talk with their hands and bodies, as well as their mouths. If a person's body language is silent and subdued it tells me a lot about his or her mental state. If someone is animated and assertive with their gestures, I know immediately how they are thinking and feeling. Nervous, fidgety actions indicate, obviously, a person who is worried or frightened about something.

Voice. I listen to people's voices. Are the words too loud, too soft? Do they hesitate, mumble, stutter? Is there hidden emotion in the strained quality of the voice?

Most people pay too little attention to their own voices, and to those of others. The sound and inflections of our voices can be wonderful tools for communicating and relating to others, or they can betray us in times of stress. By reading aloud and talking into a tape recorder, we can work on making our voices more appealing. I observe how other people use their voices, and I work daily to improve my own. I love my voice and I enjoy using it to

Improving Your Talk

effectively, expressively communicate with others.

<u>Words and meaning</u>. By listening to what people say I can detect their moods and attitudes. If their talk is gloomy, they are emotionally down. If their talk is positive and cheerful, they are. By listening to their talk I can hear it changing for the better as they continue to talk to me. My goal is always to leave people in a happier mental state than when I found them.

Among the habits I've developed that I'm most proud of is collecting things to talk about. I don't need great things to say to be a great talker, but I find it makes talk a lot easier to have a collection of very interesting things to say that I can draw from any time. My collection can include jokes, poems, aphorisms, quotations, great conversation starters, tall tales, one liners, odd facts, great statistics, current news and events–whatever I decide fits my conversational style and needs. I keep files of great things to say (even if it's only in my head), and I use items from my files frequently. I know the only way to learn great lines is to use them frequently in conversation. I enjoy pulling up neat items from my memory banks, like a magician pulling a rabbit from his hat. It's fun to show off occasionally, as long as I can help the other person look and feel good, too.

The Magic of Talk with Ben Franklin

So, in my quest to master the Magic of Talk, I work continuously to make my own talk sparkle and shine. I do this because it's fun for me, and I also like the effect my talk has on others. Every day I am astounded at the power my great talk gives me. I make acquaintances with strangers easily. I develop friendships. I change the moods and thought patterns of others. I make people happy. And, best of all, this wonderful talk brings me daily rewards: a great attitude, feelings of goodwill from everyone I meet, and success in every aspect of my life. Simply by getting out of myself and into other people, I find the world is suddenly a much happier and more fruitful place to be.

❑❑

Some inspiring affirmations that will help me improve my talk are:

I think, imagine and dream about successfully talking and socializing with others.

I build windows instead of walls; I reach out to people and invite them to interact with me.

Because I have actually worked on improving my talk, I am more skillful in personal communication

Improving Your Talk

than most people.

I keep a positive outlook all the time through positive self-talk and positive, energetic contact with others.

My new policy: no negatives ever.

People see me interacting with others and envy my fluid style and lively conversation.

I live by yes and no–yes to everything good and no to everything bad.

I am part of a vibrant network of people. I give and receive assistance and encouragement through this network daily.

I find that people are attracted to me because I provide them with friendliness, kindness, and encouragement.

I am the world's greatest listener–and that is why so many people like me.

❏❏

The Magic of Talk with Ben Franklin

Some inspiring quotations that will help me improve my talk are:

Happiness is not a state to arrive at, but a manner of traveling.
— Margaret Lee Runbeck

Bear in mind, there's no such thing as a "casual" conversation, any more than there are casual bullets in a revolver you're casually toying with in a crowded room. As long as there's one other person present, anything you say has the power to hurt or help, to lacerate or ingratiate.
— Barry Farber

Education is the ability to listen to almost anything without losing your temper or your self-confidence.
— Robert Frost

While one person hesitates because he feels inferior, the other is busy making mistakes and becoming superior.
— Henry C. Link

It is only by risking our persons from one hour to the next that we live at all.
— William James

Improving Your Talk

Life is like playing the violin in public and learning the instrument as one goes on.

– Samuel Butler

The ability to speak is a shortcut to distinction. It puts a person in the limelight, raises one head and shoulders above the crowd. And the person who can speak acceptably is usually given credit for an ability out of all proportion to what he or she really possesses.

– Lowell Thomas

One kind word can warm three winter months.

– Japanese proverb

A good way to get things started is by opening with the highest compliment you can come up with delivered squarely between the eyes of the Intimidator.

– Barry Farber

Anyone who, out of goodness of his heart, speaks a helpful word, gives a cheering smile, or smooths over a rough place in another's path knows that the delight he feels is so intimate a part of himself that he lives by it.

– Helen Keller

The Magic of Talk with Ben Franklin

If you do what you've always done, you will get what you've always gotten.

— Anonymous

I think the act of paying attention to someone else, whether through genuine interest or interest artificially contrived, is an act of kindness.

— Barry Farber

To do nothing is in every man's power.

— Samuel Johnson

Speak the affirmative; emphasize your choice by utter ignoring all you reject.

— Ralph Waldo Emerson

Tell your child, your spouse, or your employee that he or she is stupid or dumb at a certain thing, has no gift for it, *and* is doing it all wrong, and you have destroyed almost every incentive to try to improve. But use the opposite technique—be lively with your encouragement, make the thing seem easy to do, let the other person know that you have faith in his ability to do it, that he has an undeveloped flair for it— and he will practice until dawn comes in the window in order to excel.

— Dale Carnegie

Improving Your Talk

Our attitude tells the world what we expect. . . . All the people in our world reflect back to us the attitude we present to them.

– Earl Nightingale

Listening is a perversion of human nature. It must be deliberately learned. If properly mastered, listening brilliantly can move you as far forward as speaking brilliantly.

– Barry Farber

They can because they think they can.

– Virgil

Concerning all acts of initiative and creation, there is one elementary truth–that the moment one definitely commits oneself, then Providence moves, too.

– Johann Wolfgang von Goethe

If you think you can, you can. And if you think you can't, you're right.

– Mary Kay Ash

Character is the result of two things–mental attitude and the way we spend our time.

– Elbert Hubbard

The Magic of Talk with Ben Franklin

He that is of a merry heart hath a continual feast.
– Proverbs 15:15

Week Four

12

The Magic of Mixing

I am alone in my quiet sanctuary. I am very relaxed with absolutely nothing on my mind except enjoying this peaceful time with myself. I think about the progress I've made so far with the Magic of Talk program. I had no idea talk could be so simple or fun! I look back on some times when I actually took action on tips I read in *The Magic of Talk* or heard on my tapes. I recall the pleasurable feelings I had seeing my talk actually improving. I know that my talk will continue to improve as long as I listen to my tapes and allow myself to easily and comfortably follow these ideas and tips.

This week, my goal is to talk to people in groups. I know it's important to be able to socialize at parties, business meetings, conferences and other places where people come together in groups. I feel there is the potential for great power here. As Susan RoAne says working a room is one of the cheapest and best marketing methods.

As I think about the things I must do to develop my ability to socialize in groups, I see there is nothing that I can't do and nothing that is extremely difficult or stressful to do. My progress is dependent as much as anything else on my simply deciding that this is something I want to do. As Poor Richard said, "No Gains without Pains."

I have taken up the challenge because I realize I'm not going to be able to avoid socializing with people in groups, so I might as well be good at it and enjoy this opportunity for stimulating contact. I find that when I shine at meetings and social gatherings I experience a thrill, a powerful feeling that's hard to come by any other way.

The Magic of Mixing

The following are six easy steps to my development as a social networker and worker of rooms. I know if I do these six things I will improve greatly talking to others in groups.

1. <u>Schedule and attend.</u> I make it a point to schedule and attend several functions each week. And I attend each event looking my best and determined to positively work on my socializing skills. I realize that the only way I'll improve is through practice, by putting myself in situations where I want to and plan to do well.

A prelude to each function I attend is the habit I've developed of visualizing a successful outcome of the event. I recall the Chuck Norris quote, "A winner thinks about winning and a loser thinks about losing." So, I think about my participation beforehand as winning. I see myself actually at the event meeting, greeting, and talking to folks. I see myself looking great, smiling, mingling, saying clever things, and making people talk.

I see myself doing all the things I want to do at the event. I imagine who will be there and what I will say to them. In essence, I develop a picture of the outcome of the event as I want it to happen, and I see it and feel it actually happening.

I have found that this technique of mentally previewing an important event before it happens is a wonderful way to "psych" myself up and to otherwise prepare for the event. I know if I can see it happening right, it *will* happen right.

2. <u>Focus outward</u>. While I'm visualizing my successful social interaction, I see myself focusing outward at the environment, situation, and people at the event. After I've mentally prepared to interact, and taken pains to make myself look as good as possible, I don't think about myself anymore. I ignore feelings of self-doubt and uneasiness–everyone has them and why should I be different? By finding interesting things to talk about outside of me, I successfully leave the cramped confines of my skin and my head and find joy, excitement and stimulation in creatively communicating with others.

It's interesting to me the fact that I control my own happiness and success in relating to others. I recall the Abraham Lincoln quote, "Most folks are about as happy as they make up their minds to be." Since happiness is entirely a mental process, I suppose this is true. If I think I'm happy and successful, I am

The Magic of Mixing

happy and successful. And, since I can choose to think whatever I want, I do have the power to make my own happiness and success in relating to others. Eleanor Roosevelt made a wonderful statement: "No one can make you feel inferior without your consent." By the same token you can consent to feeling absolutely great about yourself and your social interactions. And as long as you think it and believe it, in your heart it will be so. I realize that as long as I have the power to think and to choose my own thoughts (which everyone does) I have the power to be successful in any realm I choose.

So, I choose to see myself successfully focusing outward at social events and meetings–being outgoing, vivacious. I choose to interact successfully with many people and to take conversational topics from the setting, the situation, the program at hand. My goal is to get others to talk to me animatedly, creatively–and to interest them with my talk. I do this by exploring various topics until I find one that ignites the other person. I make lively, witty, intelligent observations and comments. I ask questions, ask for advice they'll want to give. When possible, I give compliments and make other comments they'll want to hear.

Yes, this talking in groups is not difficult. I go into the event mentally prepared. I'm armed with a clever self-introduction and my neat supply of interesting things to say. I'm focused outward. Everything I see is a potential topic of conversation, and I make it a point to always say things that interest others, that will give them something to respond to.

3. <u>Speak</u>. It's obvious to me that nothing happens until I talk. As Barry Farber says, "accept the awesome obligation of getting things started." I do not put pressure on myself to say great things, but I do try to make my talk lively and interesting. This is not extremely difficult–it only requires me to say things a cut above the boring and the obvious. Instead of saying, "This is a great party, isn't it?" I say, "Must not be anything else going on in town tonight. Everybody is here!"

Simply speaking to as many people as possible will enable me to achieve most of my "talking in groups" goals.

4. <u>Smile and be friendly</u>. I know that generally in life we get what we give; so, if I want people to be outgoing and friendly to me, that's how I have to act toward them. Thank goodness every word I say, every

The Magic of Mixing

action I take does not have to be perfect. I've noticed many great talkers actually say a lot of absurd and occasionally incorrect things. But they are so busy acting like great talkers that we don't analyze every little thing they say. Their confidence, their talk, their smiles win us. What they say isn't half as important as how they say it.

So, I make it a point to always act like an extrovert, a great talker. And I always smile and act friendly because that's how I want people to act toward me in return.

5. <u>Circulate</u>. My goal at meetings, parties, and other social occasions is to meet as many people as possible. I see myself as a modern-day Johnny Appleseed, moving from person to person planting seeds of friendship. I talk easily and freely without having to think about how I'm acting or what I'm saying because, as William Hazlitt said, "We never do anything well till we cease to think about the manner of doing it."

I practice interacting with people in a positive, creative way everywhere I go; so, when I want to mix energetically at parties and meetings I am not using skills I don't use every day already. The talk I do at grocery stores and at banks prepares me for interactions at formal social occasions. I relate freely and easily with all manner of people everywhere. I am very proud of having this important and enjoyable skill.

6. <u>Be happy and comfortable</u>. I do my best to always be happy and comfortable in my interactions with others. I aim to try things that I can see myself successfully doing. I'm into self-improvement through talk for the long-term, and I do not have to be a perfect talker now or ever. I'm content to improve at my own pace, to progress in stages from least challenging to more challenging social occasions. I know that if I can picture myself successfully performing in a particular situation, I am ready for that situation.

I find that as I experiment with my talk that I am becoming much more confident. There are not too many situations or talk strategies that I do not feel comfortable with. After all, I am trained, now. I know more about talk than ninety-five percent of the world's population, and my talk practice is proving to me that my skills and enjoyment are improving daily.

❏❏

The Magic of Mixing

Some inspiring affirmations that will help me improve my talk are:

I am a great talker because I work at my talk every day.

I am kind and loving, and I have much to share with others.

When I shine my light on people, they glow with joy and happiness.

No one can make me feel uncomfortable or unhappy if I don't allow it.

I do what I can do within the boundaries of time, energy, and inclination.

I trust myself totally and am proud of my mental and emotional strength.

I make decisions quickly and easily, trusting that inner voice that tells me what to do.

I never hurt anyone with my words, and I don't allow anyone to hurt me.

The Magic of Talk with Ben Franklin

☐☐

Some inspiring quotations that will help me improve my talk are:

They can conquer who believe they can. . . . He has not learned the first lesson of life who does not every day surmount a fear.
— Ralph Waldo Emerson

Action may not always bring happiness; but there is no happiness without action.
— Benjamin Disraeli

That which we are capable of feeling, we are capable of saying.
— Cervantes

Every time you pat someone on the arm or shoulder, you are sending a psychic message such as "I like you," "I agree with what you are saying," "You have done well," or "All is well; don't worry."
— Leonard Zunin

Effectively communicating what you and your business are all about is not just a "plus," but an essential. Working a room can be your number one

The Magic of Mixing

marketing strategy. It's some of the best advertising you can get. . . and it's free.

— Susan RoAne

The only reward of virtue is virtue; the only way to have a friend is to be one.

— Ralph Waldo Emerson

It is the individual who is not interested in his fellow man who has the greatest difficulties in life and provides the greatest injury to others. It is from among such individuals that all human failures spring.

— Alfred Alder

If there is any one secret of success, it lies in the ability to get into the other person's point of view and see things from that person's angle as well as your own.

— Henry Ford

When I can picture myself successfully performing in a particular situation, I am ready for that situation.

— Rich Davis

Chutzpah is the cornerstone of confidence.

— Susan RoAne

The Magic of Talk with Ben Franklin

There is only one way under high heaven to get anybody to do anything. Did you ever stop to think of that? Yes, just one way. And that is by making the other person want to do it.

— Dale Carnegie

Happy is the man who has broken the chains which hurt the mind, and has given up worrying once and for all.

— Ovid

Meeting someone new can be exciting, so approach self-introduction with a sense of discovery, not disaster.

— Leonard Zunin

Don't sit down. It's absolutely impossible to work a room on your TUSH!

— Susan RoAne

If they can conceive it and believe it, they can achieve it. They must know it is not their aptitude but their attitude that will determine their altitude.

— Jesse Jackson

He who has confidence in himself will lead the rest.

— Horace

The Magic of Mixing

Nobody holds a good opinion of a man who has a low opinion of himself.

— Anthony Trollope

Of all the traps and pitfalls in life, self-disesteem is the deadliest, and the hardest to overcome, for it is a pit designed and dug by our own hands, summed up in the phrase, "It's no use—I can't do it."

— Maxwell Maltz

People often say that this or that person has not found himself. But the self is not something that one finds. It is something that one creates.

— Thomas Szasz

Men are not prisoners of fate, but only prisoners of their minds.

— Franklin Delano Roosevelt

We become what we think about all day long.

— Ralph Waldo Emerson

The greatest discovery of my generation is that a human being can alter his life by altering his attitudes of mind.

— William James

The Magic of Talk with Ben Franklin

> We are what we think.
> All that we are arises
> With our thoughts.
> With our thoughts,
> We make our world.
> — The Buddha

Seize the day, put no trust in the morrow!

— Horace

It is the mind that maketh good or ill, that maketh wretch or happy, rich or poor.

— Edmund Spencer

The movement and expressions of the eyes tell us about people. . . . Unless we *look* at others as we experience life, we miss the potentials of nonverbal communication.

— Leonard Zunin

Week Five

13

Magical Public Speaking

It's a great day to be happy and free in my sanctuary. I feel strong and content today because I know I will make myself do nothing in life that I really don't want to do.

I consider my new-found interest in public speaking. I realize everything having to do with speaking in public is not extremely fun for me. But when I close my eyes I can see myself standing before a group with a comfortable, happy expression on my face, and I see the power and rewards that public speaking brings. My occupation or career benefits enormously from my being able to communicate effectively before groups. I derive an intense personal satisfaction knowing I can handle myself in front of audiences large or small. I get tremendous joy from actually giving and completing speeches. There's something about performing before people that I like.

Yes, when I think about standing before a group, confident in myself and knowing my remarks will be well received, I feel good inside. I know this is what I want to do. That this is where I belong.

The good news about public speaking is that if I can imagine myself giving a successful presentation, I can do it. The trick to speaking before groups is to continually imagine yourself giving a great performance. I have learned that if I do not think negative thoughts about my presentations, I will not feel negatively beforehand. Worry and anxiety will disappear, and I will find myself preparing long and hard to give a winning speech, not to avoid giving a terrible one. And, this, I've found, is the mighty difference between people who excel at public speaking and those who struggle with it.

When I turn positive visualization on my speaking tasks, I find suddenly the game changes. No longer is the dominant thought "How can I survive this ordeal?" It becomes "What can I do to really knock the socks off my audience?" Once the offensive approach is taken, I find I am positively excited about the task I have before me. I spend a lot of quality time preparing for my presentation, and I enjoyably do the extra things required to ensure all goes well.

The first thing I consider when imagining how I want my presentation to go is my audience. I develop a mental image of them responding in a highly favorable way to my presentation. I see them smiling. I see them nodding in agreement. I see them taking notes and looking thoughtful in appropriate places. Most clearly of all, I see and hear them applauding enthusiastically at the conclusion of my presentation. I like the audience and it likes me. This is fun.

Next, I consider what I will say to the group that has them so inspired. I realize that it's important, even vital, to speak on the topic that the audience expects. If advance promotion has been published on my presentation, I make sure I cover the topics highlighted in the promotion.

Then, as I develop my presentation, I continually imagine the audience positively reacting to the points I make and the methods I use. After all, I'm not doing the presentation for my sake, I'm doing it for theirs. And only by pleasing them will I get satisfaction.

I am very creative in my presentation style and the methods I use to convey my message. I realize that I'm not simply a talking head, but I'm a *smiling* talking head that keeps the audience's attention by moving about, displaying energy and enthusiasm, using various visual aides and devices. I imagine how *I'd* want a speaker to get my interest, and involvement in the program, and that's what I do to get theirs. By mentally placing myself in a seat in the front row of my audience, I can easily picture what I'd want to happen. Sometimes I go to great lengths to imagine I'm a certain person with a typical understanding of the topic attending my presentation.

By moving outside of my real self and looking at my presentation in a detached way, through the eyes of another, I am able to gain fresh new insights into what should be done. Often I find that pleasing an audience is not half as tough as I imagined. The presentation does not have to be perfect. It does not have to be wonderful or earthshaking. But it should give the audience useful information, and it should do this in a lively, pleasant way. As a member of the audience, that's all I can expect. As a speaker, that's what I strive to give every time.

In preparing my speech I find it helpful to write it out first, then practice doing the speech using brief speaker's notes. I have found that it takes a few readings before I know the speech well enough to practice using the notes. Then it takes several practice sessions to be able to fluidly deliver the speech using the notes. I usually find that by the time I have gotten my speech down well enough that I feel comfortable giving it, I have the outline and the speech in my head and I can dispense with the notes altogether.

It's interesting to me now to see people give dull speeches–reading extensively, trying to recall a script word for word, or exhibiting signs of nervousness. The problem with all speakers who struggle with their presentations is the same: they have adopted the attitude that it's going to be a struggle and a grind. If they had decided to make the presentation fun and interesting, and kept that attitude throughout preparation and delivery, how would the presentation likely have turned out? A great attitude will make great things happen; a lousy attitude will make lousy things happen.

A key thought I always keep in mind is to avoid thinking about myself. By keeping my focus on what I am attempting to accomplish in my speech, and off me, I avoid all sorts of negative thoughts and images. When I go before an audience I have three things in mind: 1. The opening words I'll say to get their attention and to propel my speech forward on a positive note, 2. A picture of the entire outline of what I will say, with the assurance that when I call up a major outline heading that the supporting words and information will come, 3. The closing words I'll say to ensure a rousing conclusion and to let the folks know I'm finished. I expect a big applause when I'm done, and the only way to get it is to let the folks know I'm through.

So, I focus outward, intent on energetically and enthusiastically getting my message across to the audience. In doing this I completely bypass stage fright and all the unpleasant physical manifestations that go along with it. In giving speeches one of my principal aims is to have fun. I know that most tasks in life can be fun or dreadful, depending on how you look at them. By choosing to view public speaking as fun, I've eliminated the other alternatives and have paved the way for an enjoyable experience for all.

Finally, I trust myself and am true to myself in giving speeches. I don't try to be Dale Carnegie, Billy Graham, or Oprah Winfrey; I am quite satisfied to be myself. I use the unique abilities and strengths that I have, and I relate to each audience in a way that only I can.

I have my own program for working on and developing my public speaking. I know that the only way to improve is to practice, and I have chosen a way to get all the practice I need. This will be an exciting new adventure for me, and I expect it to be challenging, rewarding, and fun. I know what it takes to develop my speaking skills, and I am willing to pay the price in time and effort. I see public speaking as being an essential skill professional people should have, but also a ticket to a more thrilling and enjoyable way of life for me personally.

❏❏

Some inspiring affirmations that will help me improve my public speaking are:

On the topic I am speaking I am the authority and I

know how to deliver a presentation my audience will enjoy and appreciate.

The only thoughts I have regarding my presentation are positive ones. I look forward to standing before a group and sharing my topic with it.

I do whatever it takes to make my oral presentations successful.

I improve my public speaking by scheduling presentations frequently and evaluating each performance.

I have a definite plan for public speaking improvement and I follow it consistently.

I conquer nervousness by simply not allowing negative thoughts to enter my mind. I focus on the task at hand, not my emotions or fantasies of what could go wrong. When I imagine my presentation being successful I find worry disappears.

I pay special attention to visual aids and various mechanical or electronic devices I might use (like microphone or overhead projector) to ensure they are functioning properly and that I know how to use them.

Magical Public Speaking

If unexpected problems arise during my presentation, I act remarkably composed and invariably emerge from the difficulty smoothly and easily.

❑❑

Two successful professional speakers explain how they developed their skills:

I do not use notes when I go before an audience, and I haven't for years. When I gave up my notes and spoke entirely from my heart, my speaking improved significantly. I am not attached to having to please an audience, to saying it right, to anything at all. I generally meditate for a thirty-minute period before speaking, and I visualize everything going smoothly and my audience and myself enjoying and appreciating the entire experience. . . .

When I gave up my attachment to perfection about speaking, paradoxically, a kind of perfection seemed to enter into my performance onstage. The internal excitement and nervousness before speaking is my intense desire to be out there in that magical space where I am doing what I love and allowing myself to just be, and experiencing the energy flowing through me unimpeded by any attachments to the outcome. This free-flowing energy is the highest place I know

The Magic of Talk with Ben Franklin

about in the physical plane.

Dr. Wayne W. Dyer
You'll See It When You Believe It

I became an excellent public speaker because, rather than once a week, I booked myself to speak three times a day to anyone who would listen. While others in my organization had forty-eight speaking engagements a year, I would have a similar number within two weeks. Within a month, I'd have two years of experience. And within a year, I'd have a decade's worth of growth. My associates talked about how "lucky" I was to have been born with such an "innate" talent. I tried to tell them what I'm telling you now: mastery takes as long as you want it to take. By the way, were all of my speeches great? Far from it! But I did make sure that I learned from every experience and that I somehow improved until very soon I could enter a room of any size and be able to reach people from virtually all walks of life.

Anthony Robbins
Awaken the Giant Within

14

Thoughts on Self-Talk

In a book called *The Magic of Talk,* you may wonder about the emphasis I place on self-communication. What does talking to yourself have to do with talk? Everything.

We talk to ourselves every day all the time, whether we realize it or not. In fact, what you do in a day's time is largely based on the nature of your self-talk. If your talk is along the lines of "I feel great, this is my day. Everything I touch today is turning to gold," how do you think your day will go? If, on the other hand, you say to yourself, "Gee, I must have gotten up on the wrong side of the bed. Everything I touch today breaks. I feel like I'm losing it." How do you think self-talk like that will make you feel? How effectively will you interact with others? What will be your level of productivity?

The obvious question now becomes "Can we actually control our thoughts?" Think about it for a second. If we *can* control our thoughts, doesn't this mean we can have a super, never-quit, highly enthusiastic attitude all the time? Yes! And, if we have this great attitude at all times, won't this mean we'll go through life happier and with much more success? It's likely. And, doesn't this great attitude mean we'll get along better with other folks, find more joy in all of our communication with our fellow beings? Most definitely!

So, let's return to that vital question, the most important question in this book. Can we control our thoughts? The answer is an unequivocal *Yes!*

My goal now is to prove to you finally and forever that you can change your attitude by changing your thoughts. Probably the simplest way to do this would be for me to ask you to reflect back on your life and recall several times you did this.

Have you ever successfully controlled your anger? I hope so! Most mature adults (and many younger folks, too) have learned that being angry is

Thoughts on Self-Talk

not fun and seldom helps a situation. Therefore, they make a conscious decision to curb the emotion when they detect it getting out of control.

Have you ever toned down your excitement? Increased your enthusiasm? Put on a happy face?

You might find it helpful at this time to reflect on several specific instances where you pumped your emotions up, toned them down, or changed the way you were thinking in some fashion. It's very important that you realize you can do this and that you are already doing it.

The method most of us use to control our moods and emotions is called self-talk. When you receive a Publisher's Clearinghouse notice that you have won a grand prize, you likely say to yourself something like, "Oh, brother, here's another one. Let's don't spend the money until we have the check in hand." You deliberately tone down your emotions because you know you probably haven't won ten million dollars, although the announcement seems to proclaim you have.

Say you're parked at a stoplight and a teenager putting on her lipstick gives your car a good jolt when her foot slips off the brake. Before you get out of the car to check for damage, you likely pause for a moment to gain self-control. You say something to yourself like, "Don't be too hard on her. You've done some stupid things in your time, also."

We've all encountered people who don't think but simply react to everything. Those folks, let me tell you, are out of control. They make life miserable for everyone around them.

So, it's often the words we say to ourselves that control the thoughts we think, the emotions we feel, and the actions we take. If these words are consistently positive, happy, upbeat, cheerful, assertive and gay—we will be. If they are sad, depressed, fearful, and gloomy, guess what? Yep, that's how we'll feel. And, the results we get in life won't be what we want.

The fact is if we speak to ourselves in a positive, supportive and happy way all the time, most of our life's troubles will disappear. Remember, happiness is a mental state; it exists entirely in our brains. Personal happiness is helped by a good job, lots of money, great health, loved ones; but it can be achieved without any or all of these. Happiness can also be elusive for people who have everything. Look at Janis Joplin, John Belushi, Elvis Presley, Marilyn Monroe. Didn't they have it all?

Unfortunately, many of us have been taught by our parents, or learned in school or on the playground, *not* to have positive self-talk. How many times as you were growing up did you hear the

Thoughts on Self-Talk

words "No! You can't. Not yet. When you are older. Stay in the yard. Eat your spinach!"

Many of us got bleaker messages than these programmed into our brains. Some parents say cute little things like "What's wrong with you? Why do you keep doing that? When will you grow up? I can't wait until you are old enough to move out."

Now what do those messages repeated a million times do to a person's self-esteem? What happens is the child repeats mentally the words the parents say. If a parent says, "What's wrong with you?" when the child makes a mistake, the child will say the same thing to himself when he misspells a word in class, or strikes out in a baseball game. "What's wrong with you, dummy? Can't you do anything right?" My father innocently told me, "You should have your head examined." (If most children's heads were examined I'm afraid what would be found would be an endless tape recording of negative messages.)

Thus, what's needed for many of us is reprogramming or, to continue the analogy of the tape recorder, a new tape. I'm convinced that right thinking and happiness can be achieved simply by changing your self-talk. And self-talk can be changed by hearing the right messages over and over and over.

Think about it, negative self-talk is developed over the years. One negative thought can have disastrous results, but imagine the destructive forces of *decades* of negative thinking. It's no wonder we have so many folks totally dysfunctional in this country—on drugs, in prison, living off welfare, addicted to alcohol.

What I propose is to replace the negative tape with a positive one—literally. I believe what is needed is to hear endless positive thoughts in your head, in your own voice. That's the rationale behind the Magic of Talk transcripts, and that's why I hope you'll give them a try.

The following are a few additional ways you can fill your head with positive thoughts, images and self-talk:

Tapes: Listening to any audio tape with an uplifting message is an excellent way to fill your head with positive thoughts. Many great communicators I've met use self-help and motivational tapes.

I have discovered that I can make my own tapes of books and other written material at a tiny fraction of what they would cost retail. This allows me to make a great tape on any subject for the pennies it costs for a blank tape. Also, I am able to

Thoughts on Self-Talk

select the exact message I want to record, and I get the wonderful benefit of hearing it in my own voice. If you are interested in self-improvement, I urge you to make your own tapes. You'll find that as long as you select passages you like, that have a positive tone and a useful message, you can hardly go wrong.

Reading material: If you have read this far in this book I assume you appreciate the value of reading for self-improvement. Reading positive, uplifting material can also influence your self-talk. Collect books that make you feel good when you read them. Several of my favorite authors are: Ralph Waldo Emerson, Henry Thoreau, Dale Carnegie, Norman Vincent Peale and Wayne Dyer.

Reading "downer" materials can also bring you down. I have gotten into the habit of avoiding certain stories on the front page of my daily newspaper: obviously my self-talk is not bolstered by reports of stranglings, throat-cuttings, and child abuse that the editors seem to think I need to know about. Similarly, I have found that reading the sports page and following teams on TV does not help my positive outlook. Since I have no control over the Atlanta Braves, the Dallas Cowboys, or the Chicago Bulls, what good does it do for me to root for or against them?

Graphic representations: There are many ways you can boost your self-talk and thoughts through images you create and post on your walls, mirrors or doors.

    1. Success collage: The term collage means an artistic composition of materials pasted on a surface, usually with a unified message or theme.

    The success collage technique, as I first read about it in *Science of the Mind*, November 1991, involves cutting out words and pictures from magazines and pasting them onto a large sheet of poster board. These words and pictures (plus anything else that seems appropriate, including your own artwork, photos, whatever) should depict scenes that represent what you want to happen. The success collage works much like a billboard or a TV commercial. If you see the message often enough, you will want to buy!

    2. Flow chart: In *Wishcraft : How to Get What You Really Want* Barbara Sher describes how she creates flow charts to help her visualize step-by-step what has to be done to achieve her goals. Flow charts are a graphic way of helping you think, to figure out contingencies, to plan. By making large, colorful flow charts and posting them on your wall, you can easily "see" your dream as you make it

Thoughts on Self-Talk

happen.

Quotations: I am extremely fond of positive quotations, as you may have noticed in reading this book. Everyone should keep a scrapbook of favorite inspiring or instructive quotations. These "gleanings" can be used anytime to stimulate us and charge our self-talk.

One of the best self-made tapes I have is a recording of *Dale Carnegie's Scrapbook.* One Sunday afternoon I sat down and read the book, which is a collection of Carnegie's favorite quotations, into my tape recorder. Reading those positive, inspiring words for two hours supercharged me. Since then I have enjoyed and profited from the tape many times.

He that can compose himself, is wiser than he that composes books.

15

In Conclusion: Rich

I hope you have enjoyed and profited from this book, and will continue to do so for many years to come. I imagine it would be impossible not to derive some gain from this book and the exercises it contains, if the right mental attitude were maintained. Ah, that's the problem for many people. They go into a program trying to force themselves to do it, or they don't believe in their hearts they can do it. Either way, they sabotage their efforts. Ben and I encourage you to use the Magic of Talk program with the right mental outlook–that is, approach the activity from a feeling of strength. Keep a relaxed, positive attitude. Trust yourself to be true to yourself and what you want out of life. Feel deep in your soul that you will always do the thing that is right for you. Most of all, plan to have fun!

I suppose there may be a few passages in the transcripts that do not pertain to goals you have for yourself. Feel free to reword the transcripts, or rewrite large parts of them. Your goal should be to feel as positively as you can about the messages you are attempting to implant in your mind. I believe that whatever you put on tape and replay repeatedly you will act on; so, make adjustments as needed to the transcripts.

A very interesting book called *Total Mind Power* by Donald Wilson, MD explains ways to use taped transcripts to lose weight, stop smoking, lower blood pressure, improve memory and to make just about any other change you might desire. Once you have gotten benefit from the Magic of Talk transcripts, you may wish to write others that address other needs in your life. If so, *Total Mind Power* would be an excellent resource. At this time *Total Mind Power* is not in print, but your local library should be able to help you locate a copy. It's worth the trouble.

I have enjoyed traveling on this journey of self-improvement and discovery with you. Please let me

In Conclusion: Rich

know if you find the program fun and useful. If you have suggestions for improvement of *The Magic of Talk* for future editions, I would like to receive them, also. Write to me, Rich Davis, in care of MerryMount Publications, Post Office Box 6428, Asheville, NC 28816.

*Tho' Modesty is a Virtue,
Bashfulness is a Vice.*

16

In Conclusion: Ben

This is a glorious time to be alive. I remember writing to Joseph Priestley around the year 1780: "The rapid Progress *true* Science now makes, occasions my regretting that I was born so soon. It is impossible to imagine the Height to which may be carried, in a thousand years, the Power of Man over Matter. We may perhaps learn to deprive Masses of their Gravity . . . . Agriculture may diminish its Labor and double its Produce; all Diseases may by sure means be prevented or cured, not excepting even that of Old Age. . . ."

The Magic of Talk with Ben Franklin

I now have the opportunity to observe closely the magnificent changes that have occurred in the world since I last trod here. You have conquered gravity; you have much more than doubled the produce of agriculture while greatly diminishing its labor; you have cured many diseases. But you have also brightened the night sky with electric light. You have invented machines for speedy travel over land, underground, across and beneath the oceans, through the sky, and into outer space! You have split the atom and sent spaceships to the farthest reaches of the solar system.

Yes, this is a great time to be alive, and I have much reading and observing to do to acquaint myself with all the advancements that have been made. The thing I look forward to most, though, is talking to people. As ever I am curious about the problems, hopes, dreams, and daily habits of others. I find that through two hundred years of time the one thing that hasn't changed is the fascinating variety of human beings on the planet. People still pursue money, happiness, comfort, sex, friendship, and diversion much as they did in my day. The biggest thrill in the world these days is the same as it was two hundred years ago: making contact with another person in a vital way. I trust that this little volume will provide you with a way to explore other people more

In Conclusion: Ben

enjoyably and skillfully than ever before. If Rich and I have done our jobs well, you should soon be reaping a multitude of rewards from your contact with others.

For now, I am content to explore this world and its people and to grow old again. Then, who knows, maybe I'll break out the Madeira wine and the giant cask and try my little experiment again. In another two hundred years maybe Americans will be populating the stars and Ben Franklin will have *his* picture on the dollar bill.

The Magic of Talk Diary

This section is for folks who want to get immediate benefits from *The Magic of Talk* but are not interested in a formal plan. Use this section of the book to record specific times during your day that you used and profited from a suggestion from this book. Note the date and action taken in the space provided. By developing the habit of recording positive steps you take, you will reinforce these desired actions. Soon, you will find you will take these steps without needing reinforcement. The new behaviors will become a part of your life.

Date   Action
_____
_____
_____
_____
_____
_____
_____
_____
_____
_____

The Magic of Talk Diary

Date   Action

The Magic of Talk Diary

Date   Action

The Magic of Talk Diary

Date   Action

Recommended Reading

Dale Carnegie's Scrapbook, Dale Carnegie, Dale Carnegie, Dale Carnegie & Associates, 1959.

How to Win Friends and Influence People, Dale Carnegie, Simon & Schuster, 1936.

You'll See It When You Believe It, Wayne W. Dyer, Avon Books, 1989.

Making People Talk, Barry Farber, William Morrow & Company, 1987.

The Autobiography of Benjamin Franklin, Benjamin Franklin, any edition.

Creative Visualization, Shakti Gawain, New World Library, 1978.

How to Work a Room, Susan RoAne, Warner Books, 1988.

Awaken the Giant Within, Anthony Robbins, Simon & Schuster, 1991.

Unlimited Power, Anthony Robbins, Simon & Schuster, 1986.

Total Mind Power, Donald Wilson, Berkley Publishing Corporation, 1978.

Enroll in the Magic of Talk Class!

You like the Magic of Talk but you want the support of a master instructor to help you through the program. No problem. Take the Magic of Talk class!

You'll receive a copy of The Magic of Talk with Ben Franklin, a class instruction booklet, plus six lesson assignments which you can complete at your own pace.

Each lesson will be examined, evaluated and returned to you promptly. Currently Rich Davis is the master instructor for all students, and he provides personal, professional and caring instruction.

To Enroll: Send $95.00 (check or money order only) to Magic of Talk Course, P.O. Box 6428, Asheville, NC 28816. Phone (704) 251-2628. Satisfaction guaranteed.

Book Ordering Coupon

Please send me ___ copies of The Magic of Talk with Ben Franklin. I have enclosed $12.00 (check or money order only) per book which includes postage and handling.

Name _____

Address _____

City/State/Zip _____

Send to: MerryMount Publications, P.O. Box 6428, Asheville, NC 28816.

About the Authors

Rich Davis is a public speaking teacher at Shaw University Educational Center in Asheville, North Carolina. He has written over three hundred articles and columns which have been published in a variety of periodicals. Rich is an avid Toastmaster and has completed the Dale Carnegie Leadership Course. He has a Ph.D. in adult education and an M.A. in English.

The two loves of Rich's life are writing and speaking. Since Rich discovered the Magic of Talk he has become a man possessed, traveling the country talking about talk. Sometimes he brings his pal Ben Franklin along.

Ben Franklin is one of the original founding fathers. Author, scientist, businessman, and diplomat, Dr. Franklin has returned from a two hundred year hiatus. Currently he is touring the country with Rich Davis to provide entertaining training on two vital topics: The Magic of Talk and The Magic of Reading.

By the way, for skeptics who do not believe in the magical properties of Madeira wine, the experiment with the flies did occur and Ben did successfully revive two of them.